Color – Amaze

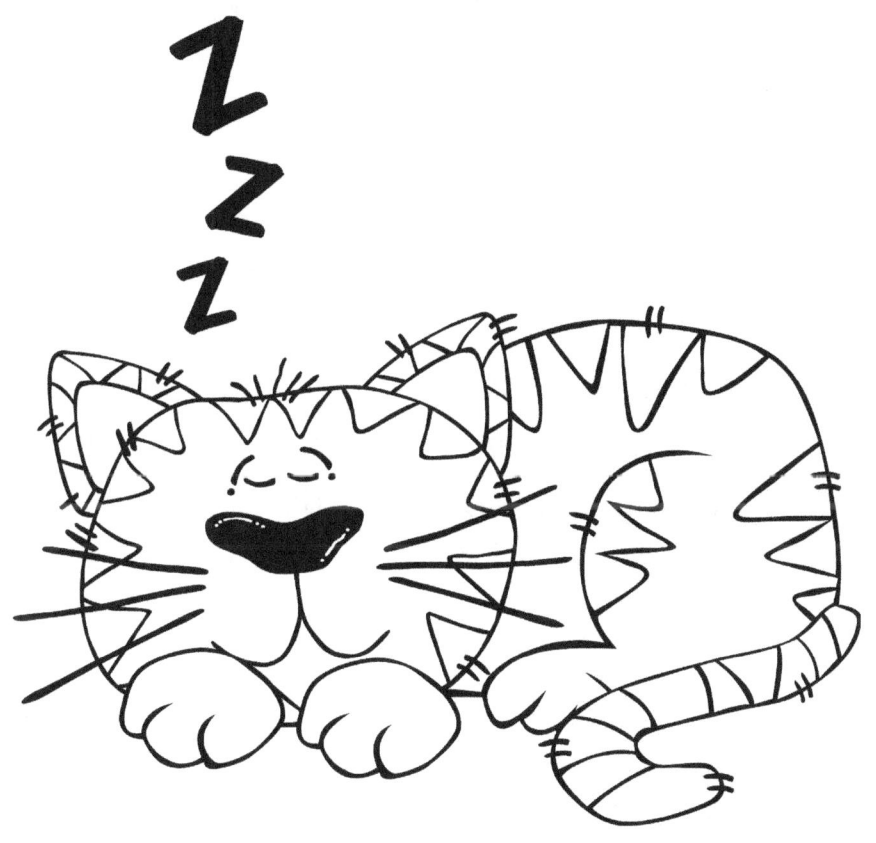

By Megan Marchese

Copyright Megan Marchese

ISBN-13: 978-1533365958

ISBN-10: 1533365954

This Book is Dedicated to:

Being a kid again.

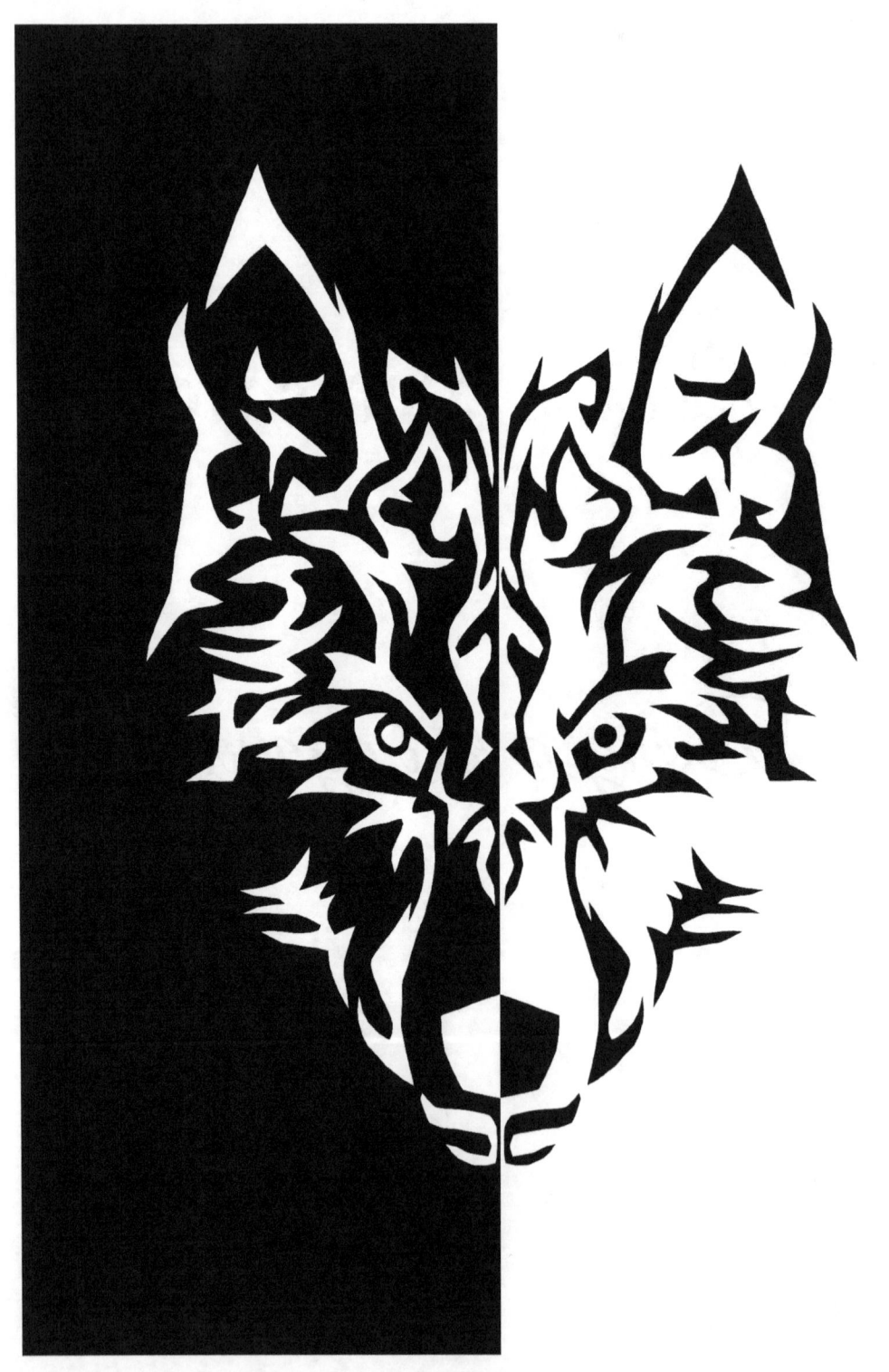

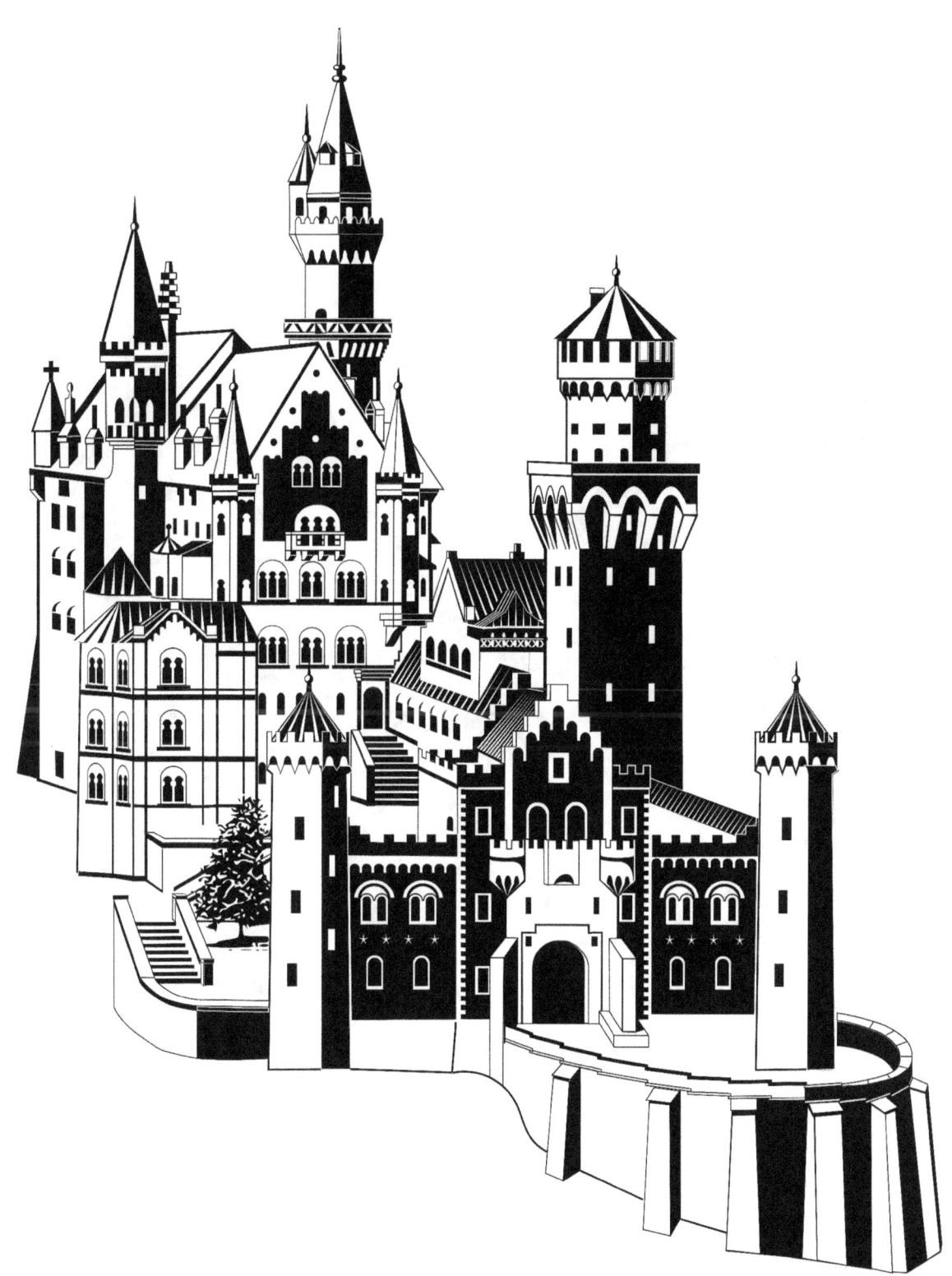

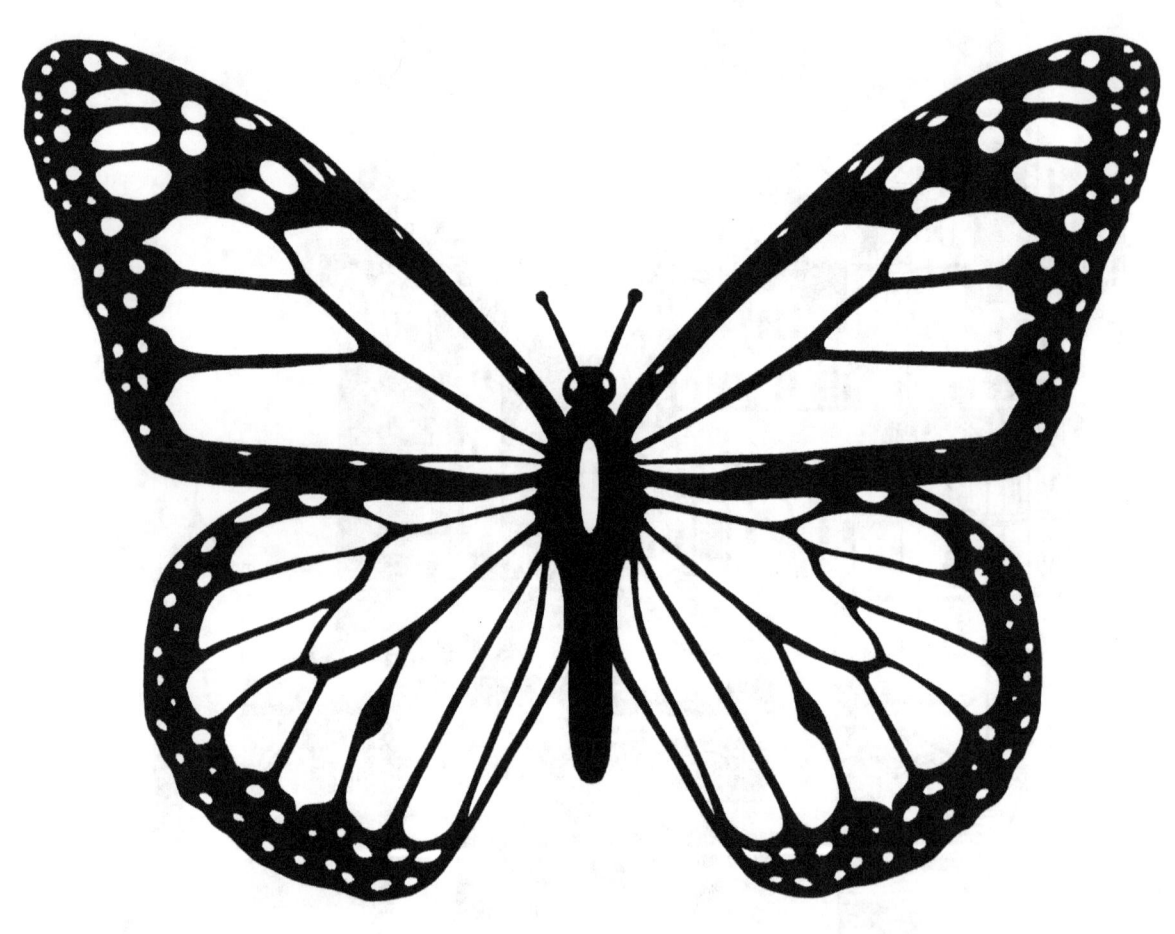

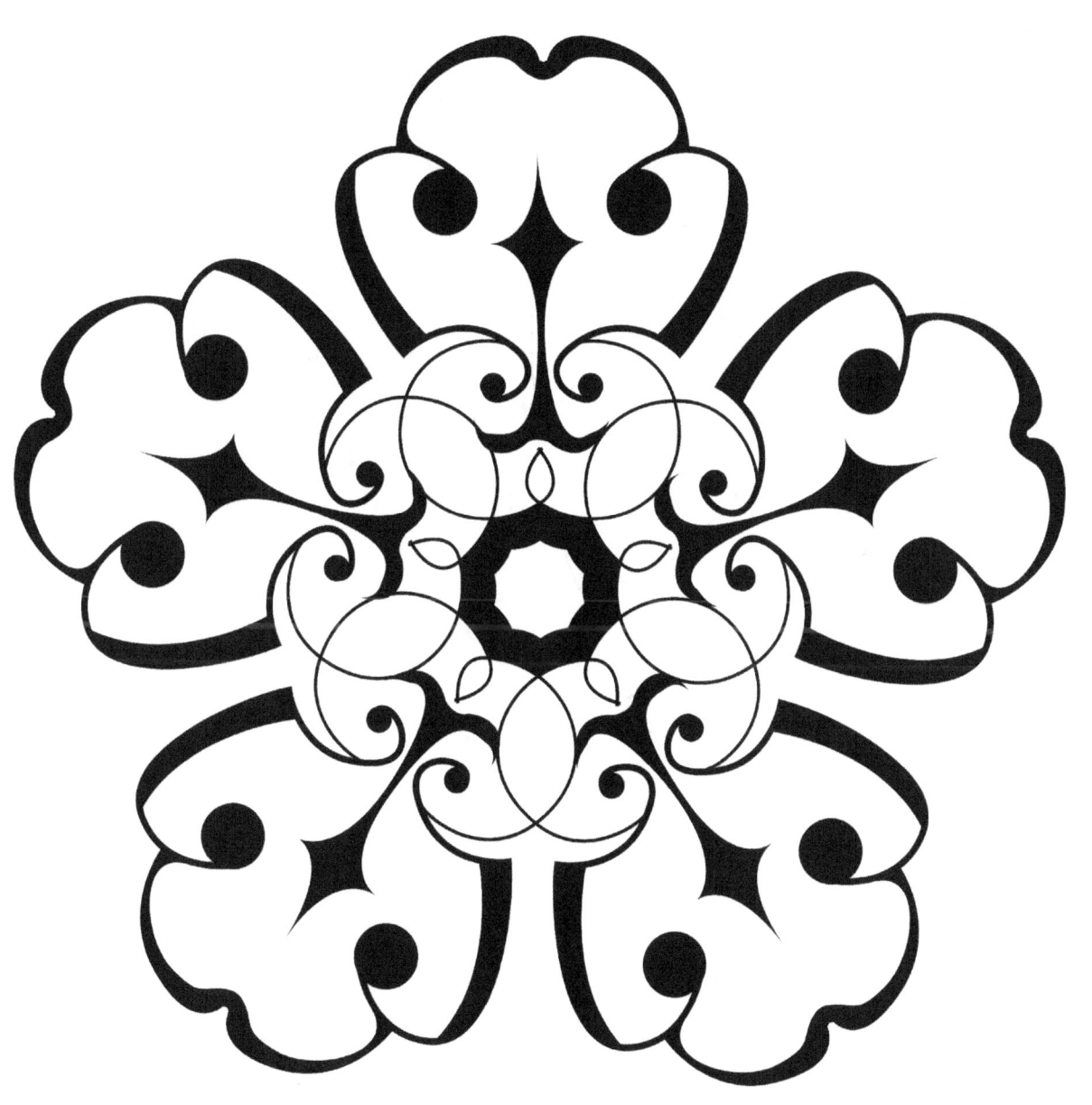

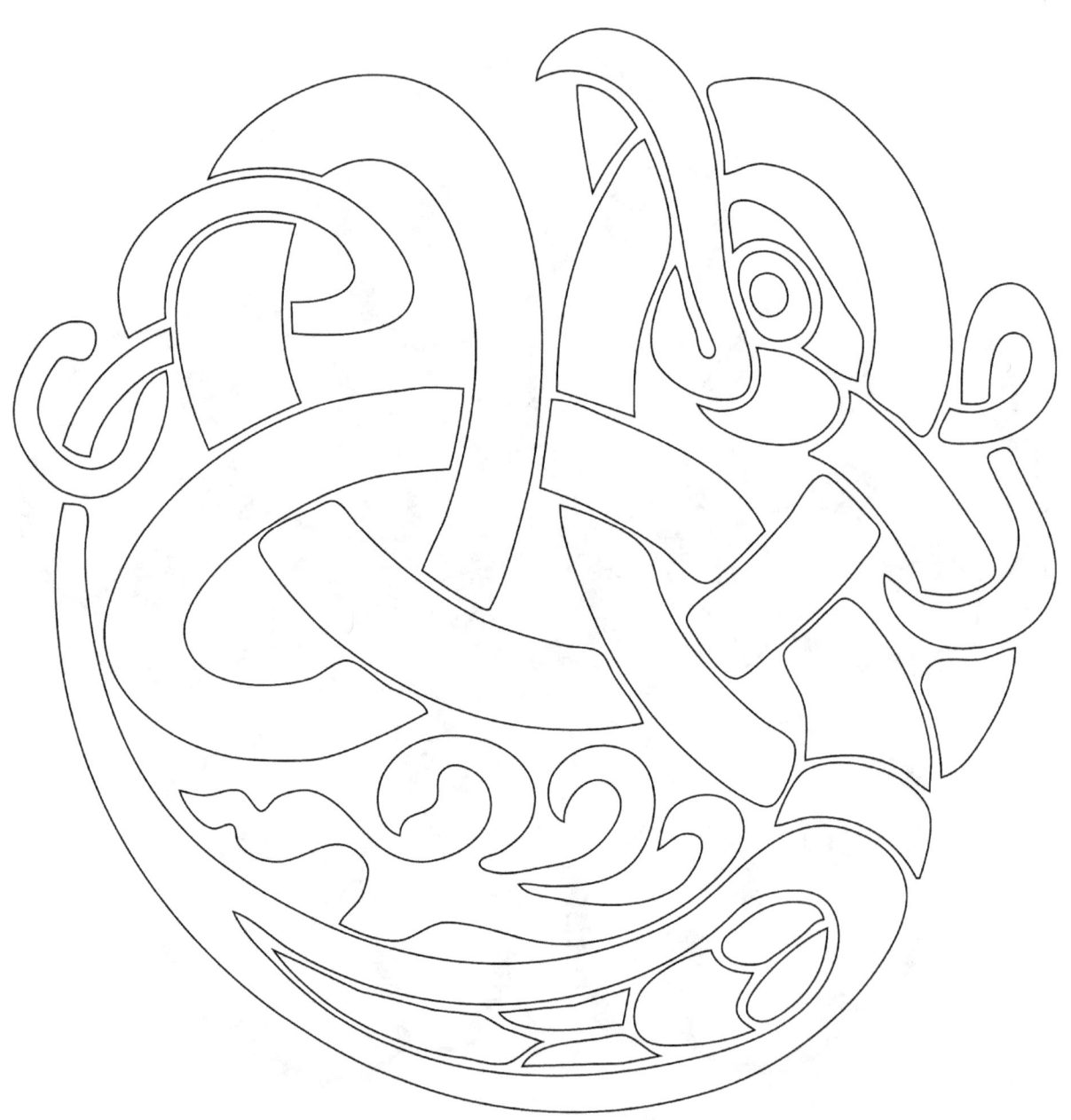

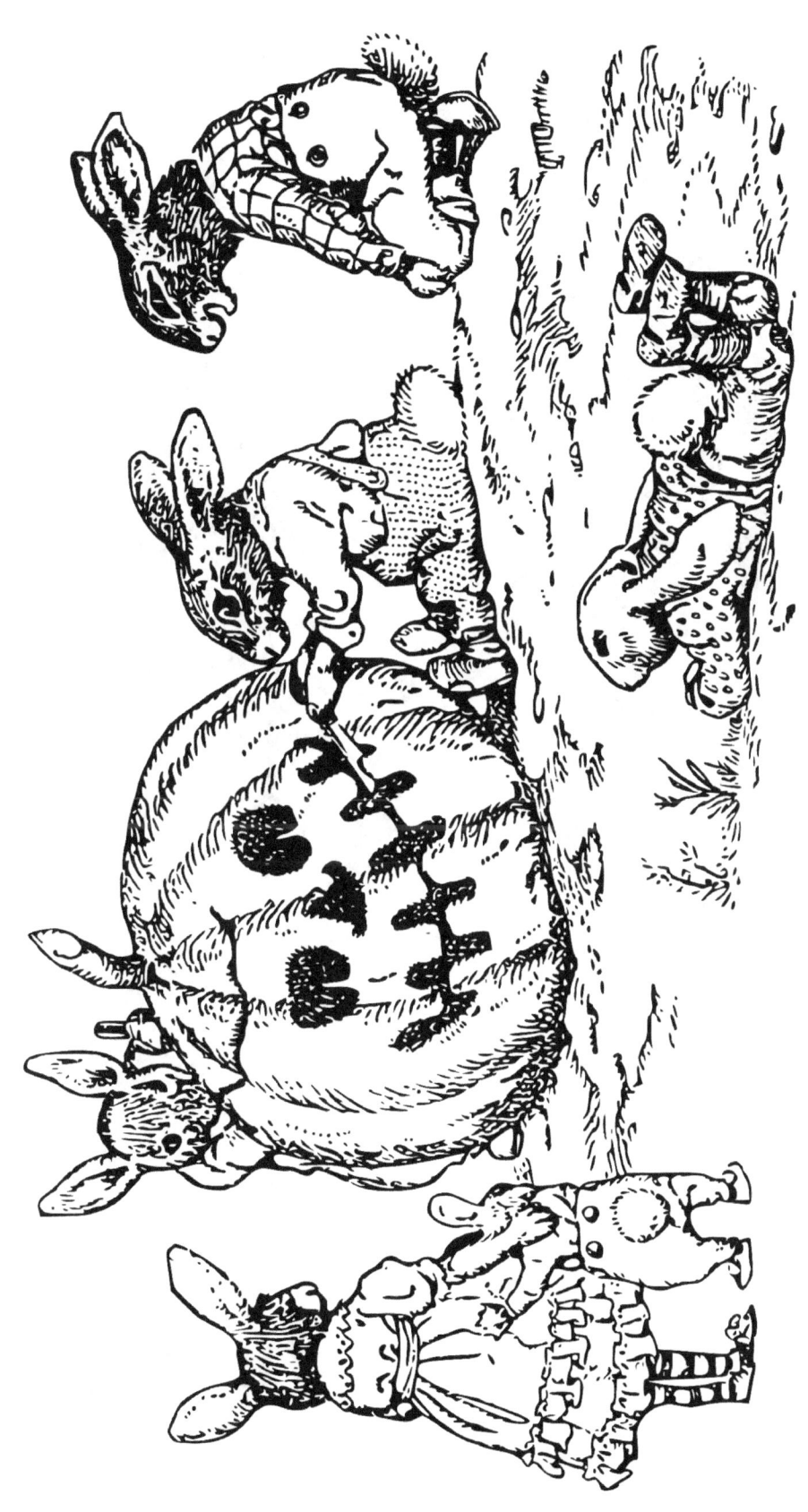

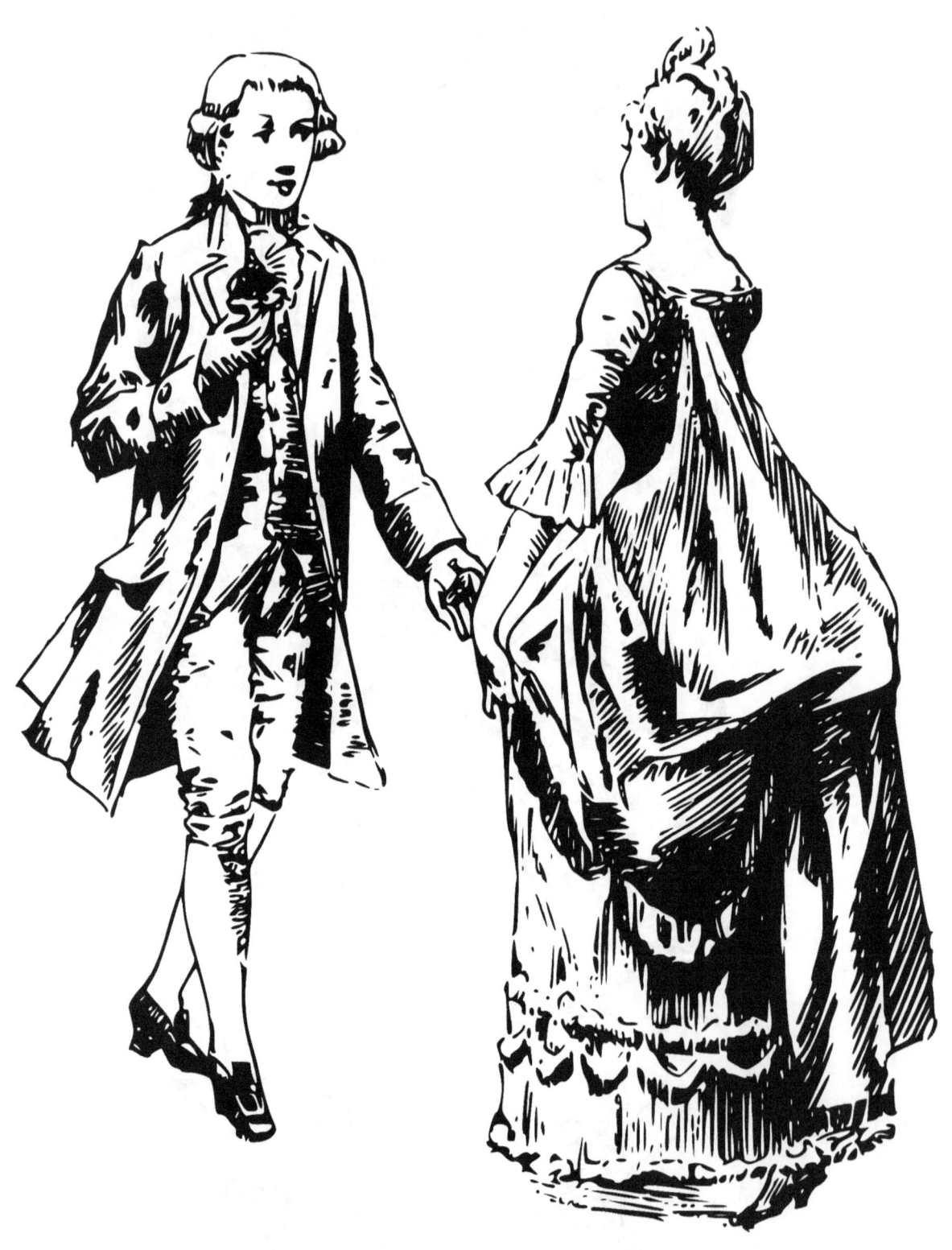

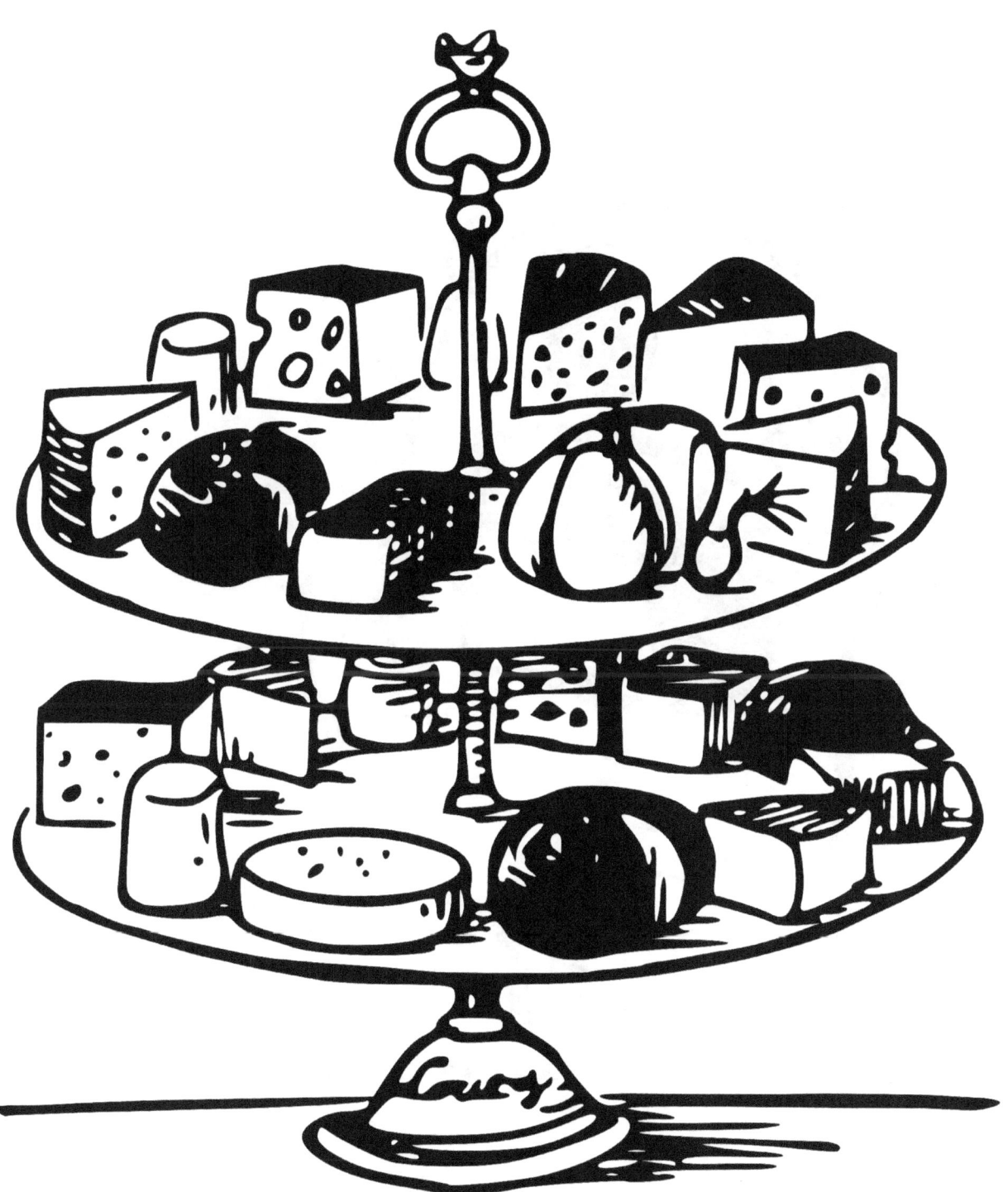

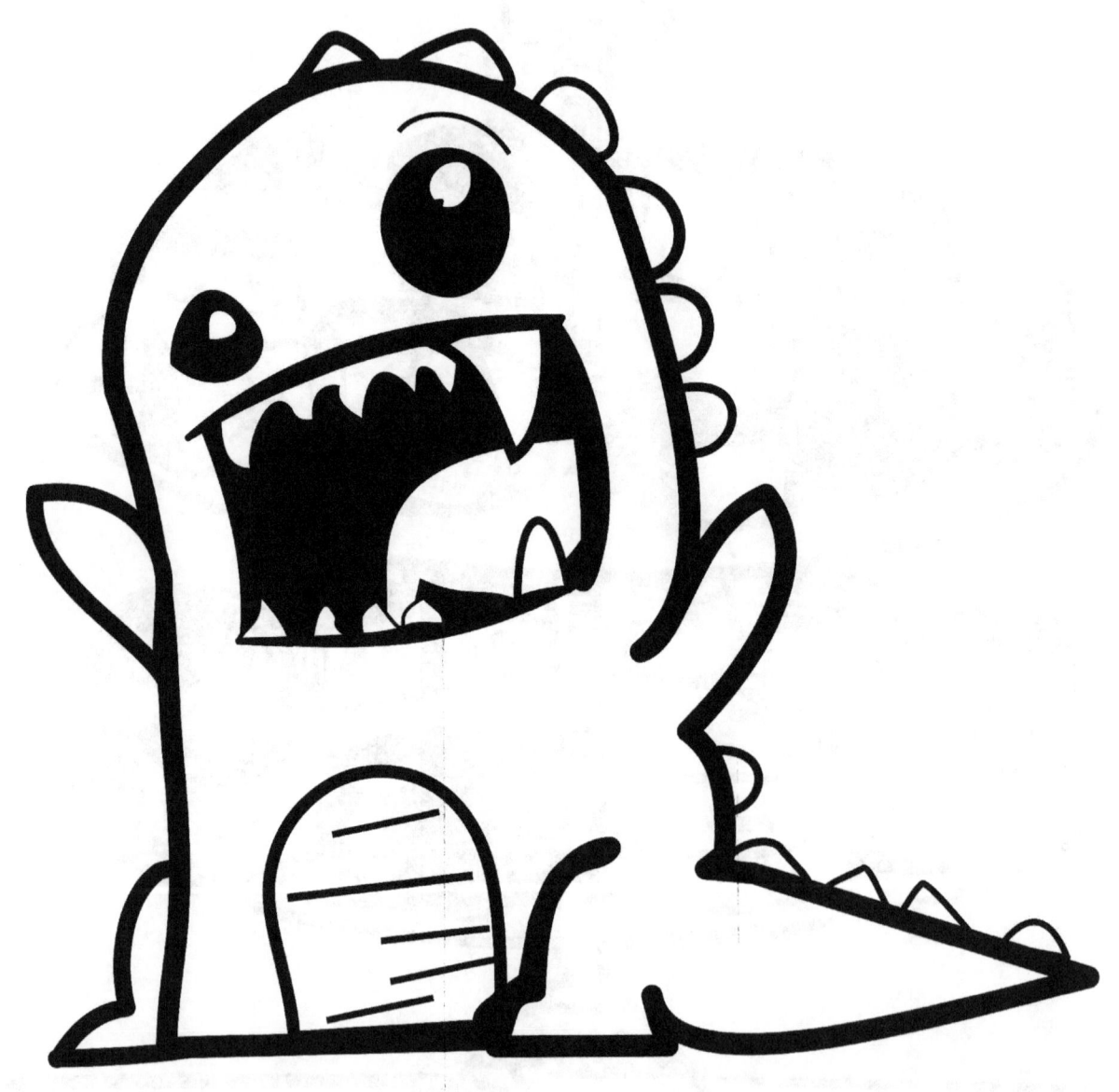

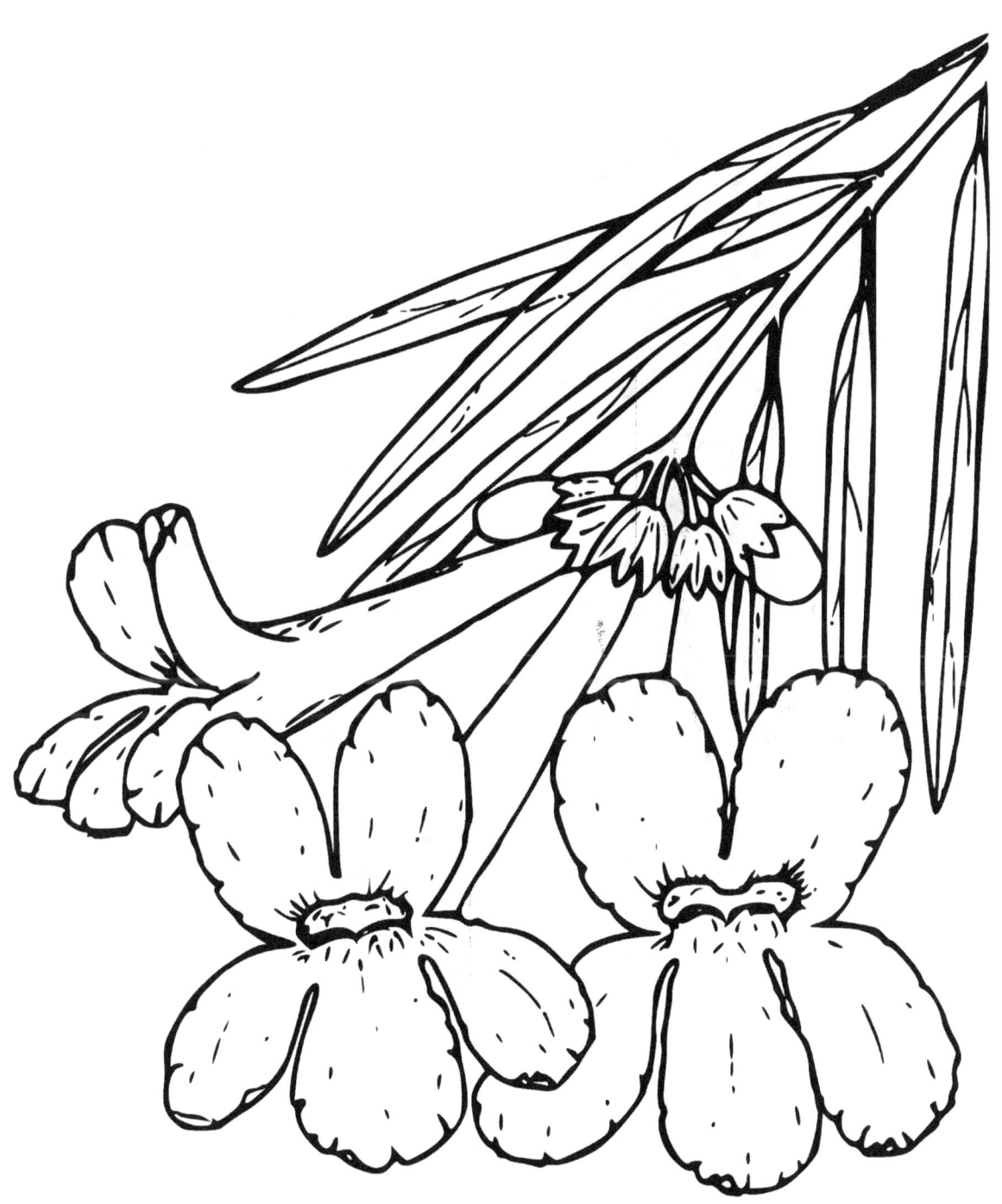

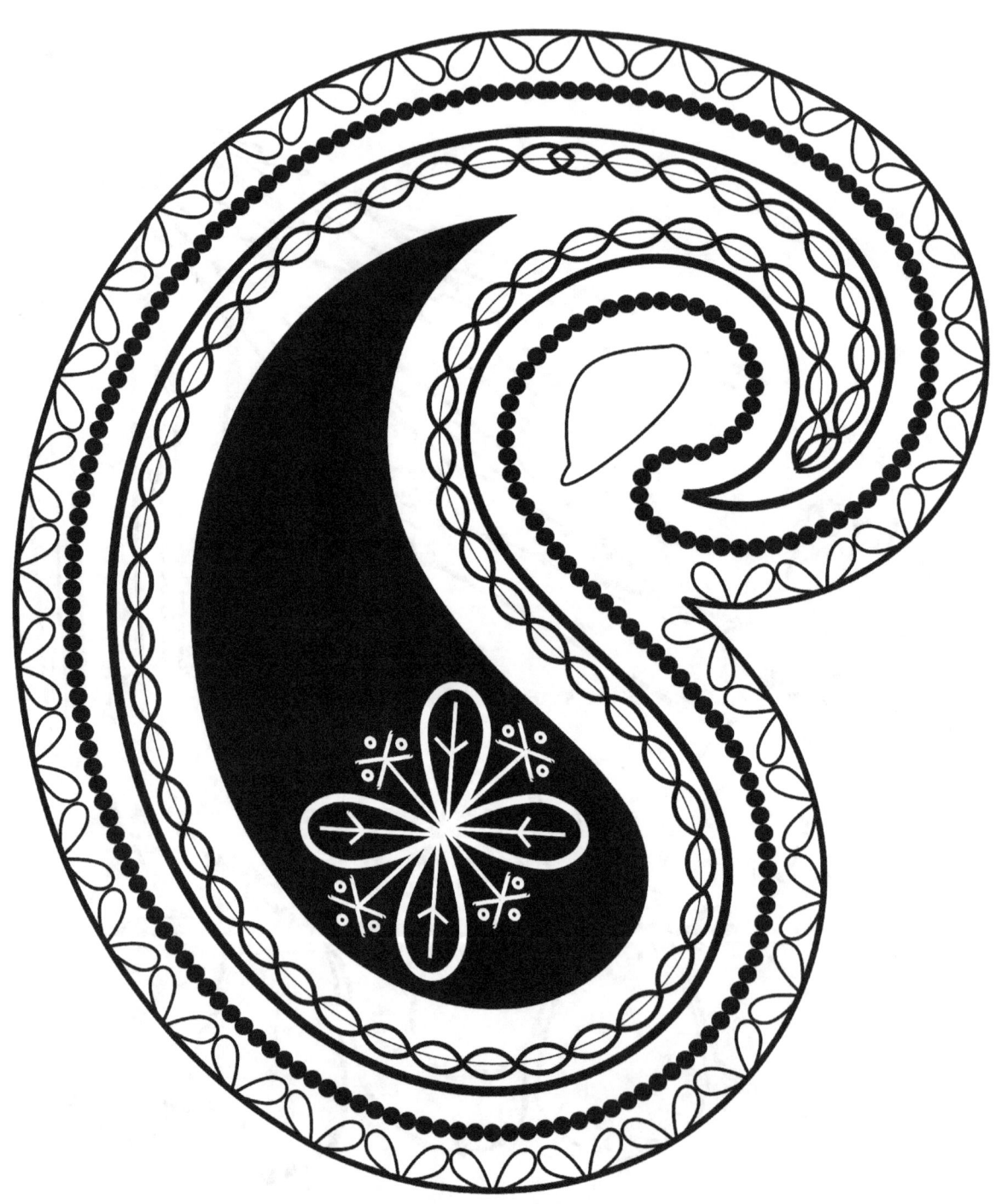

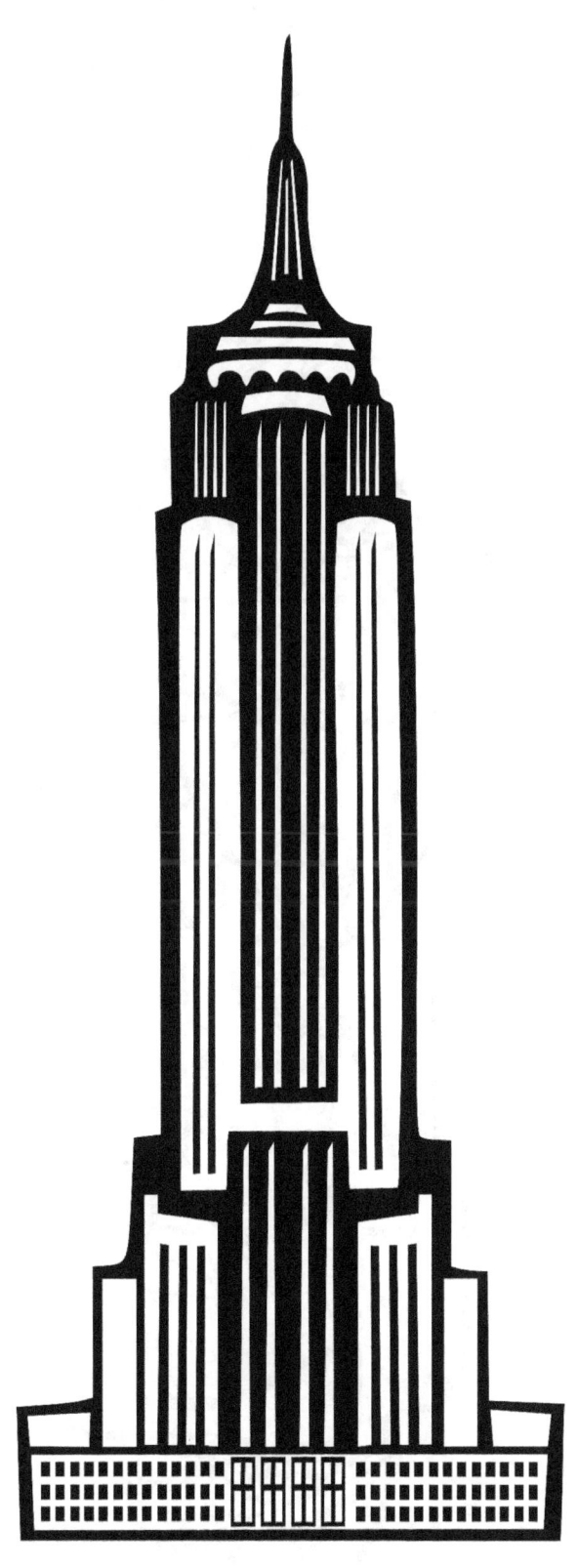

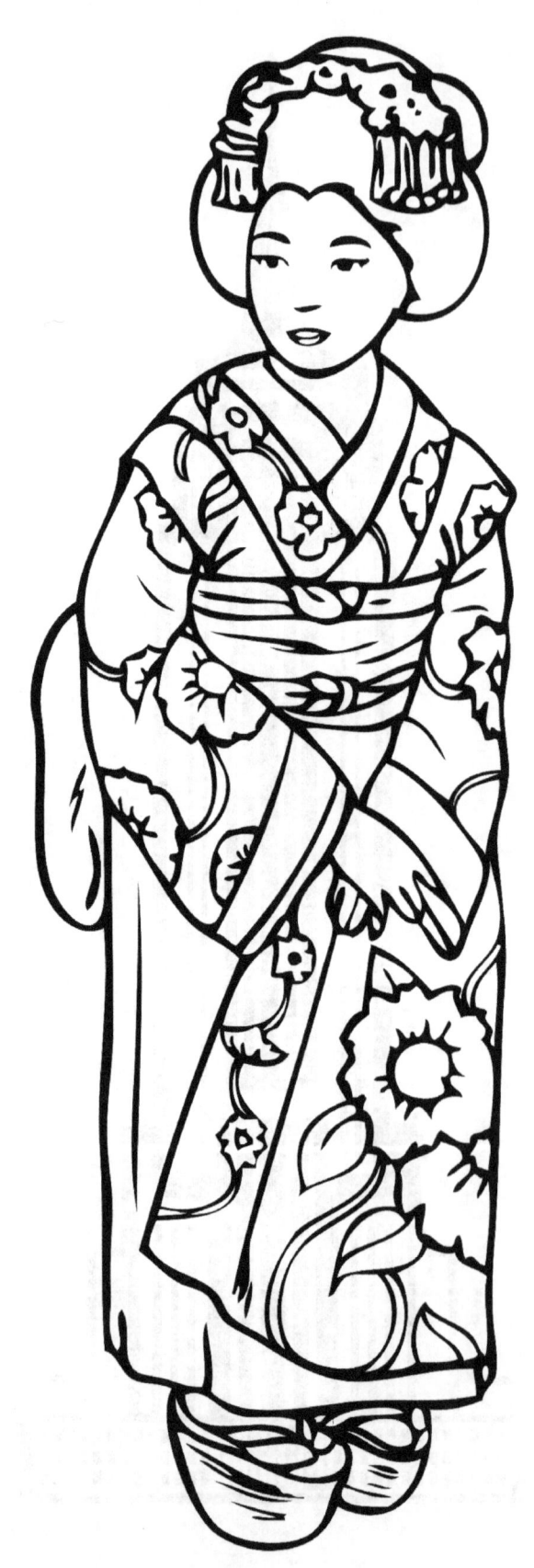

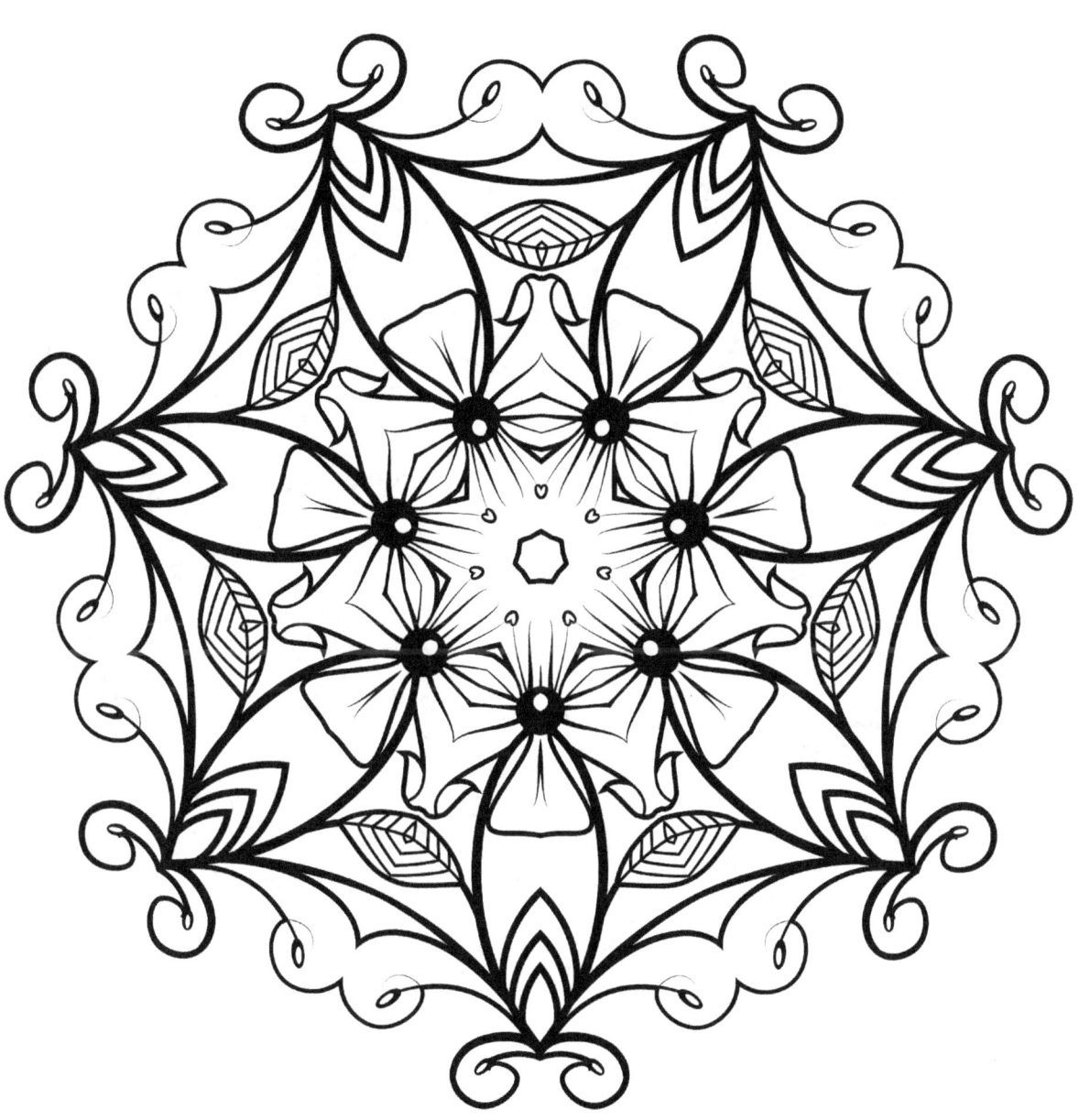

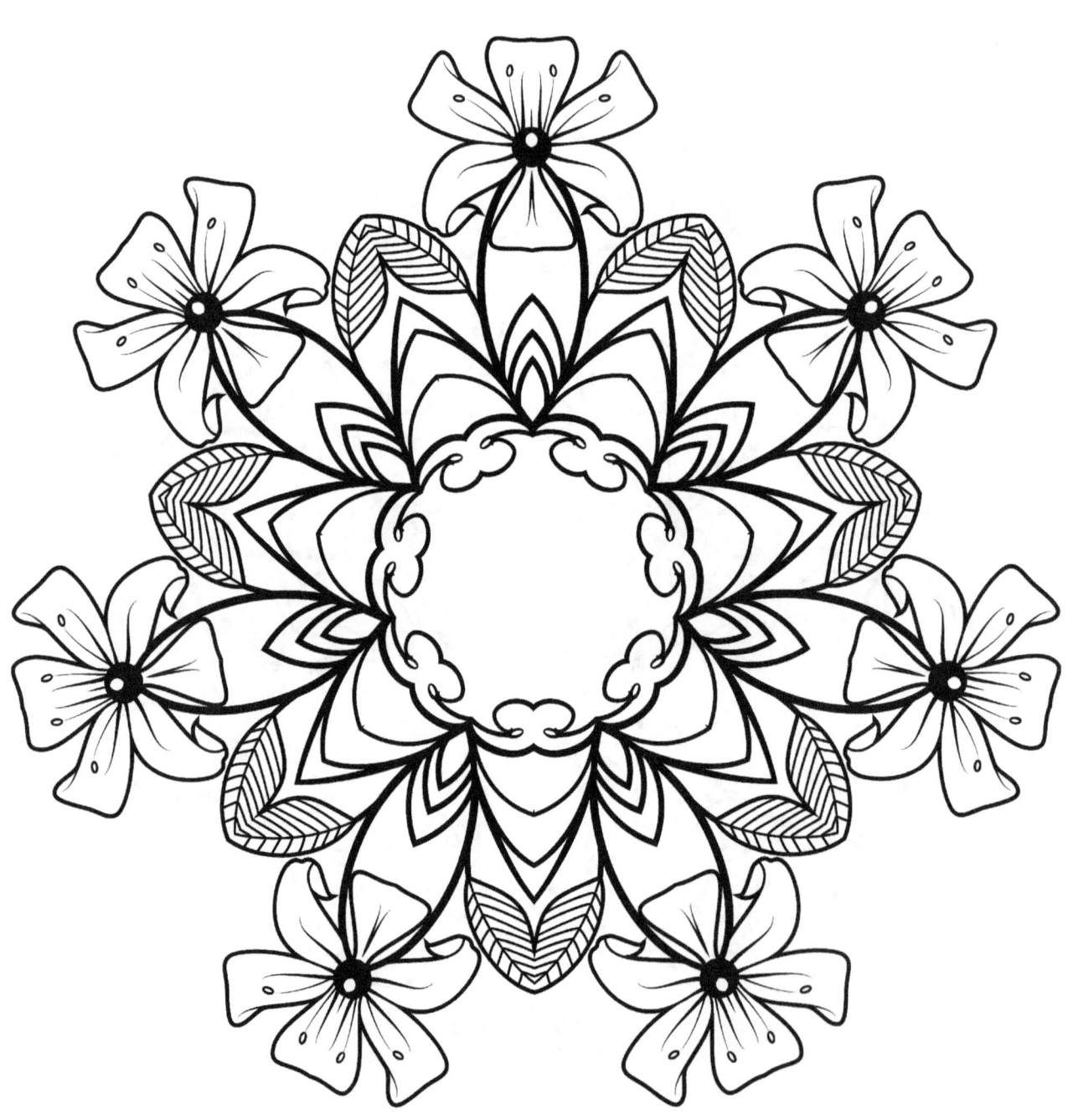

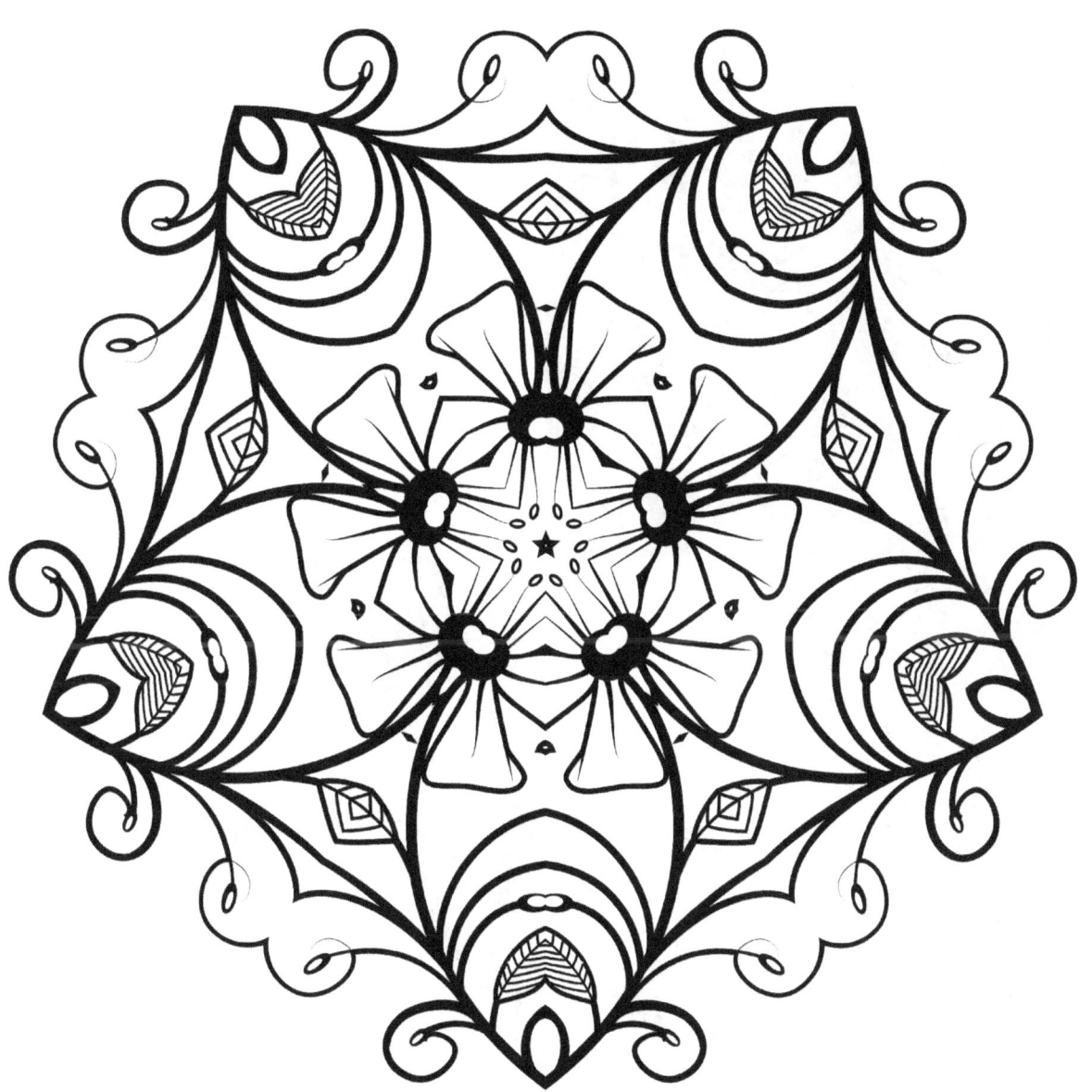

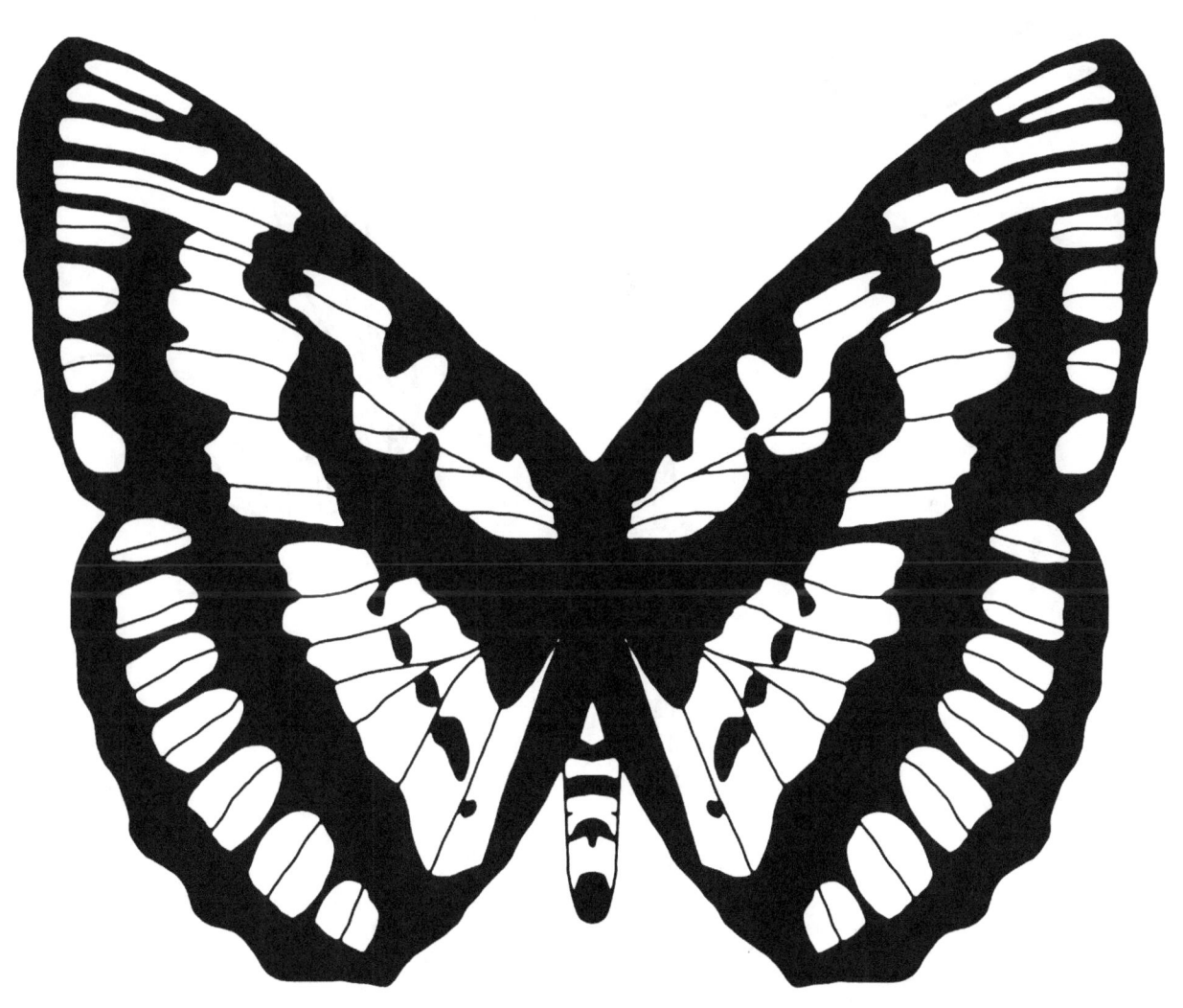

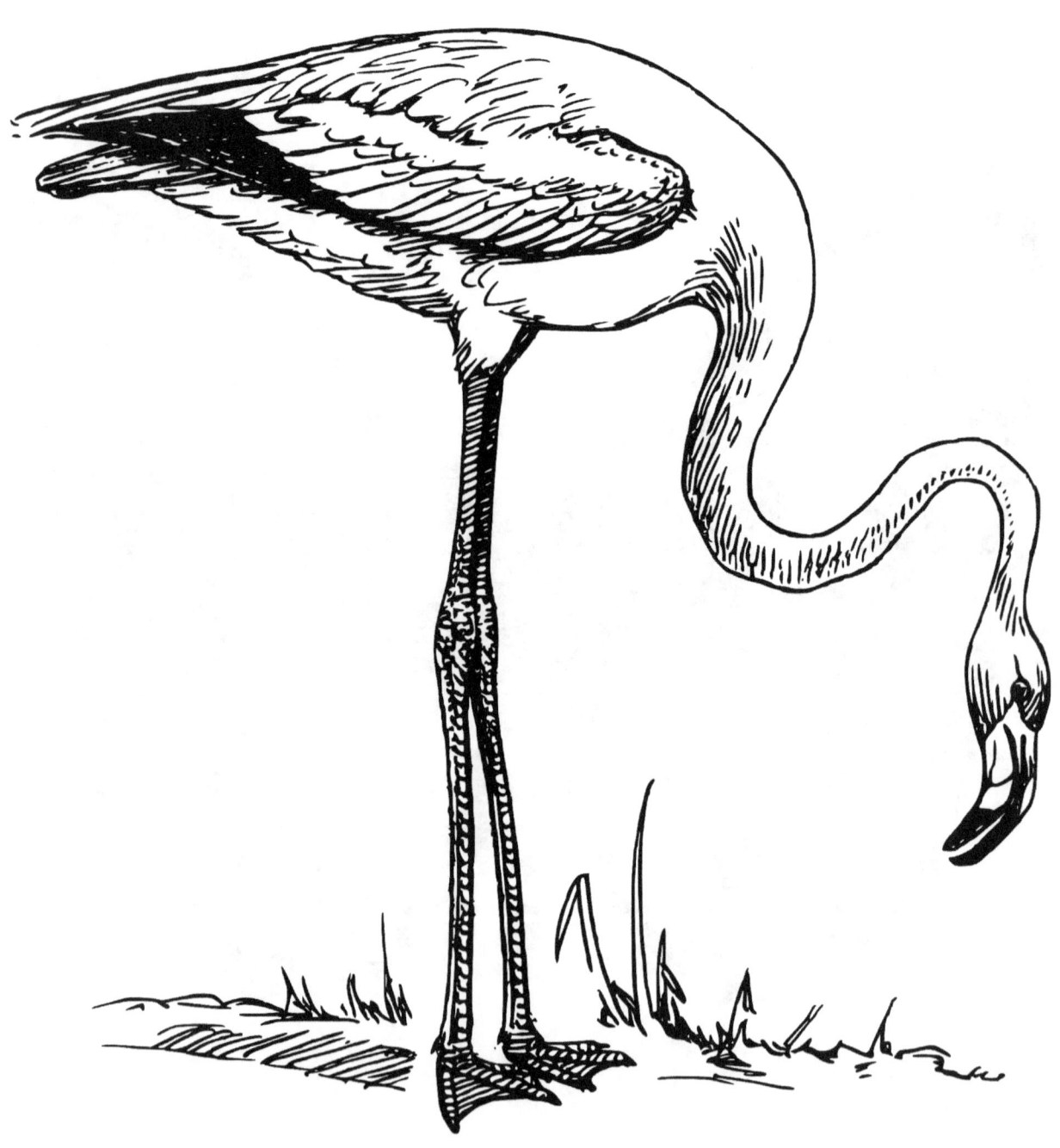

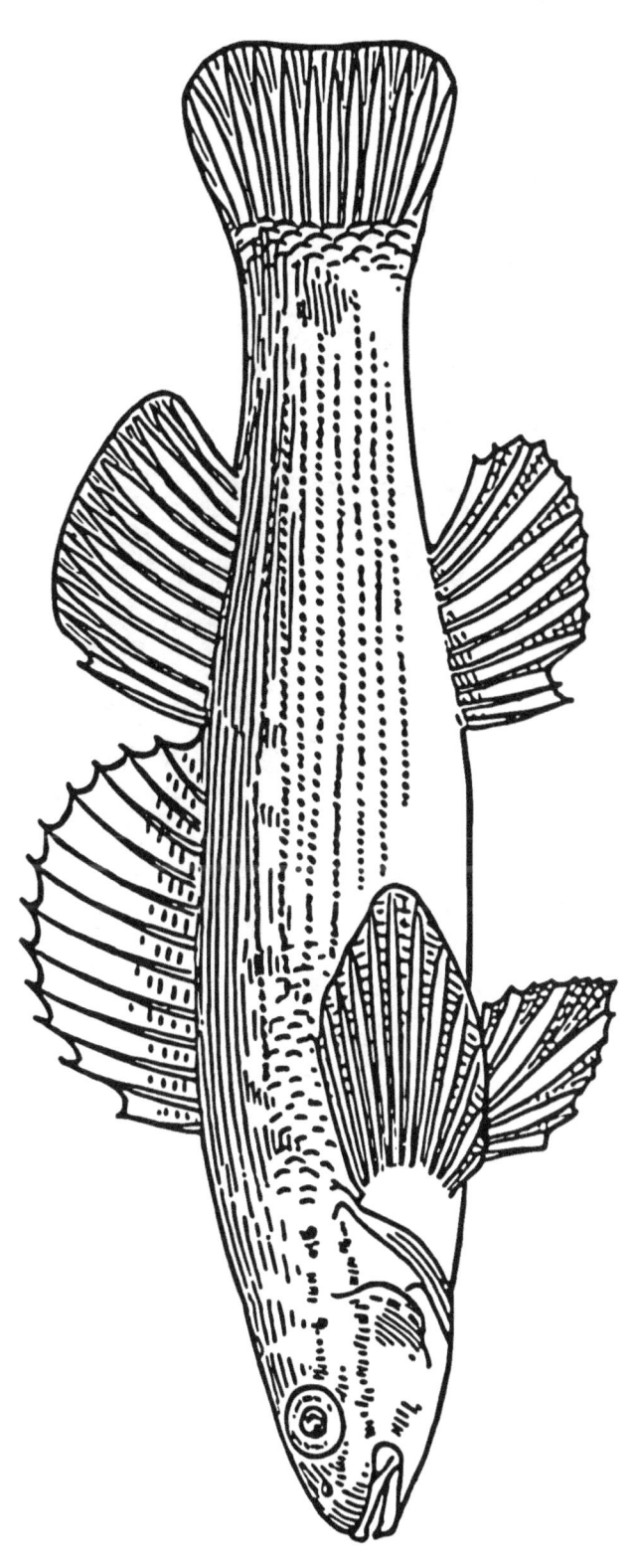

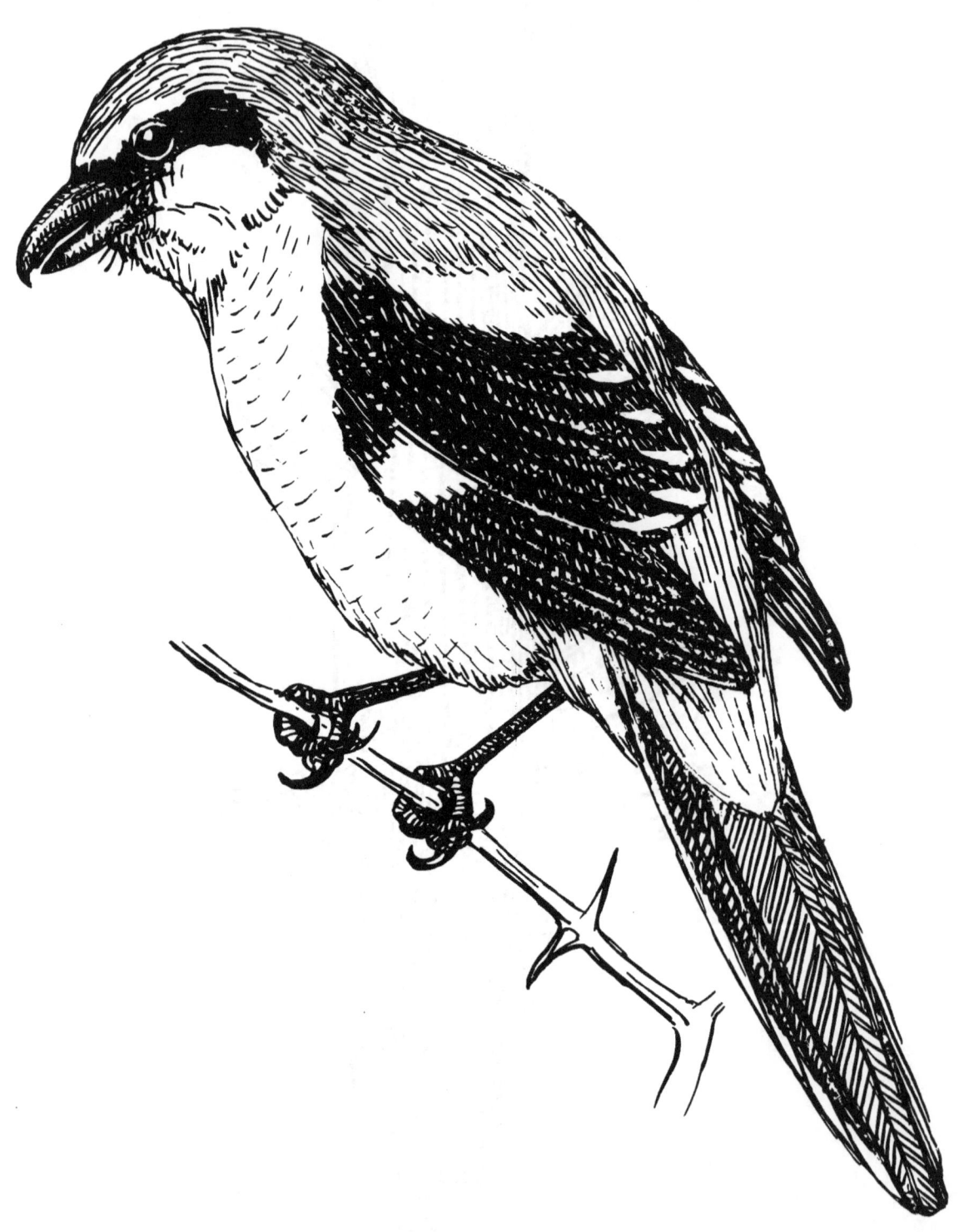

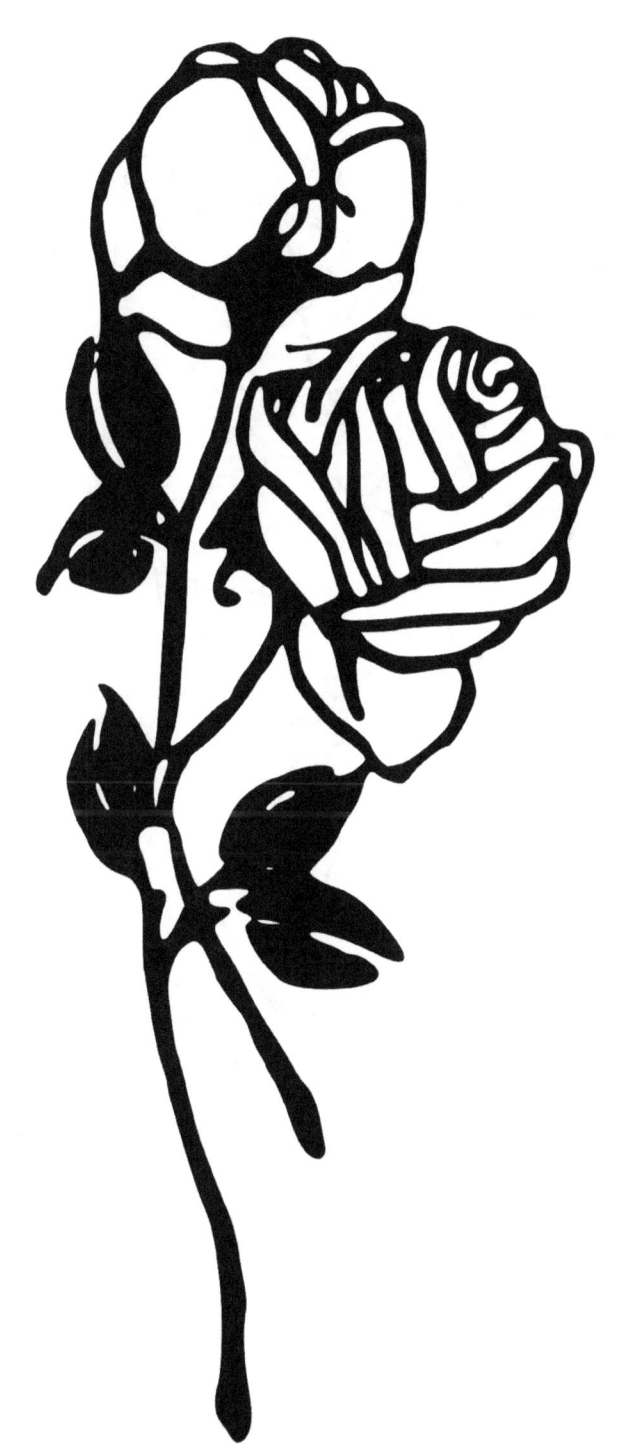

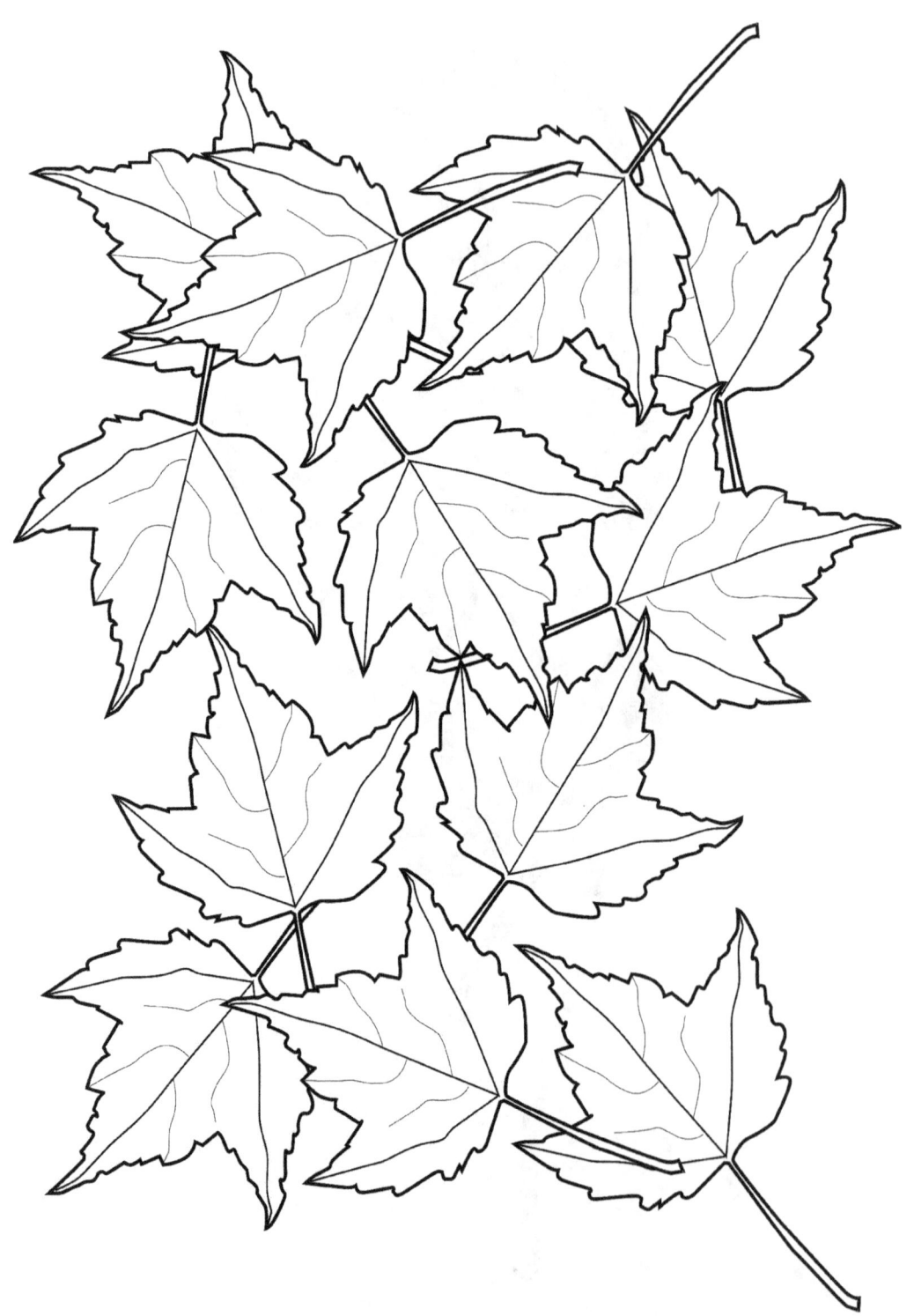

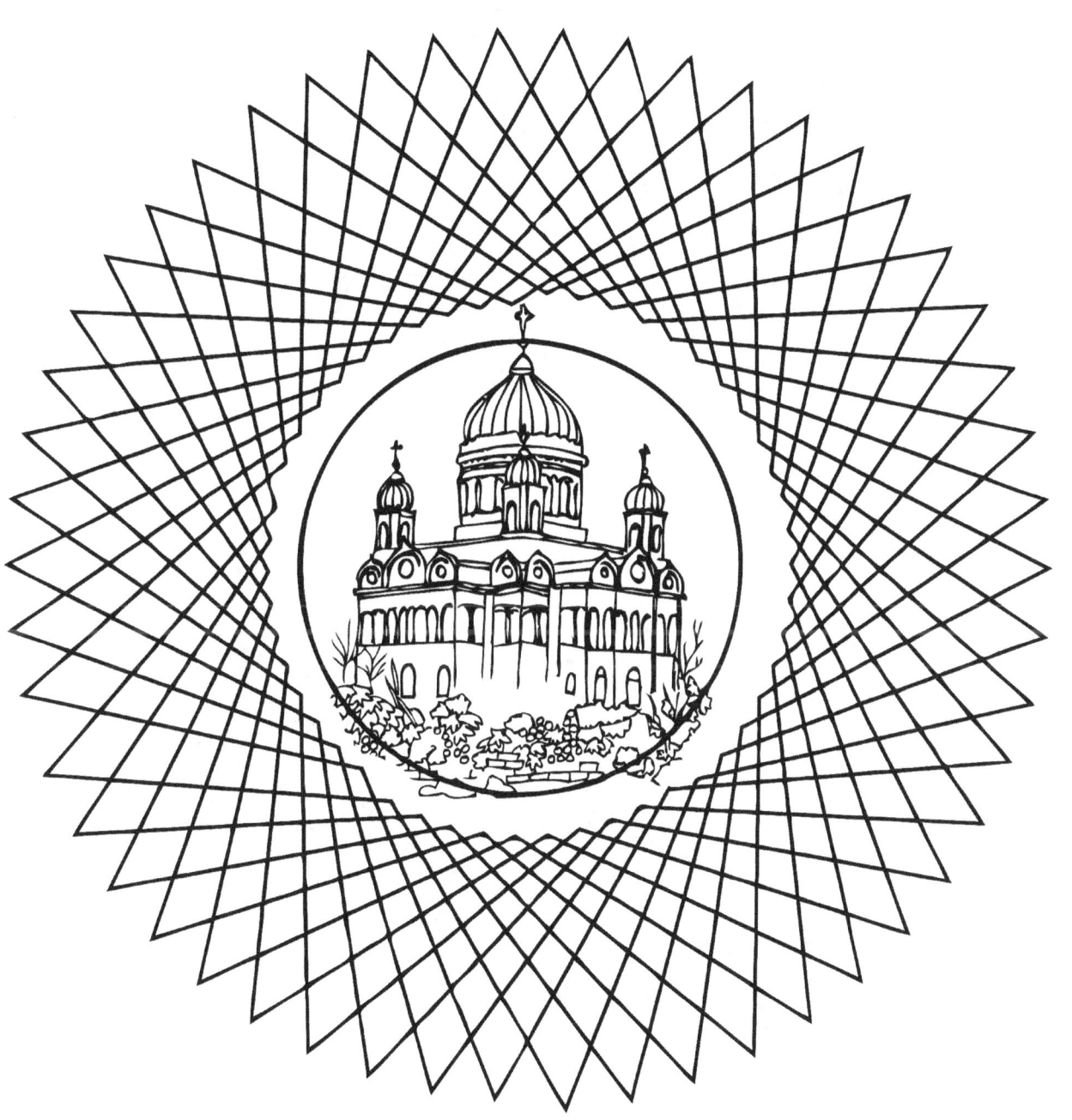

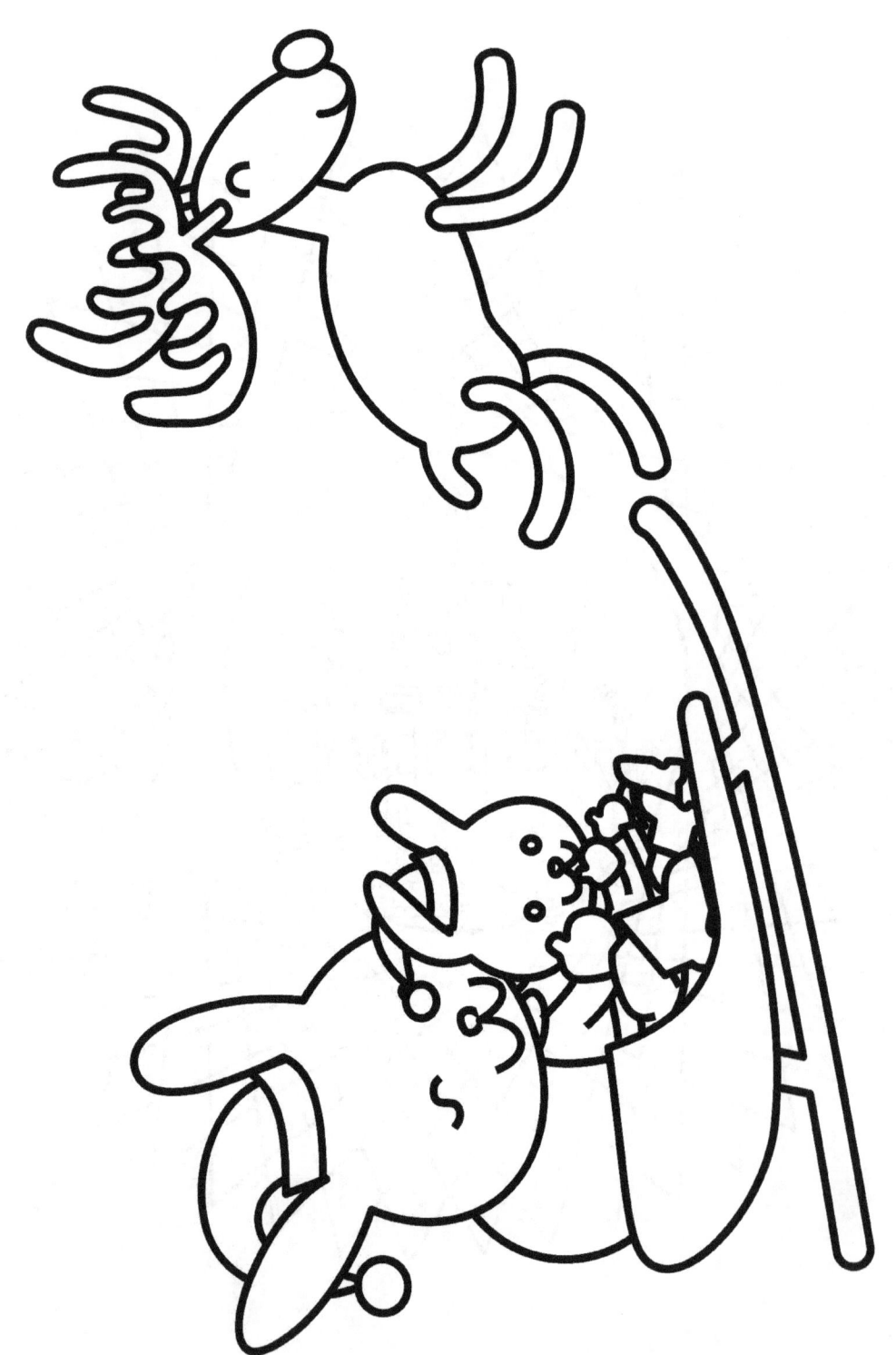

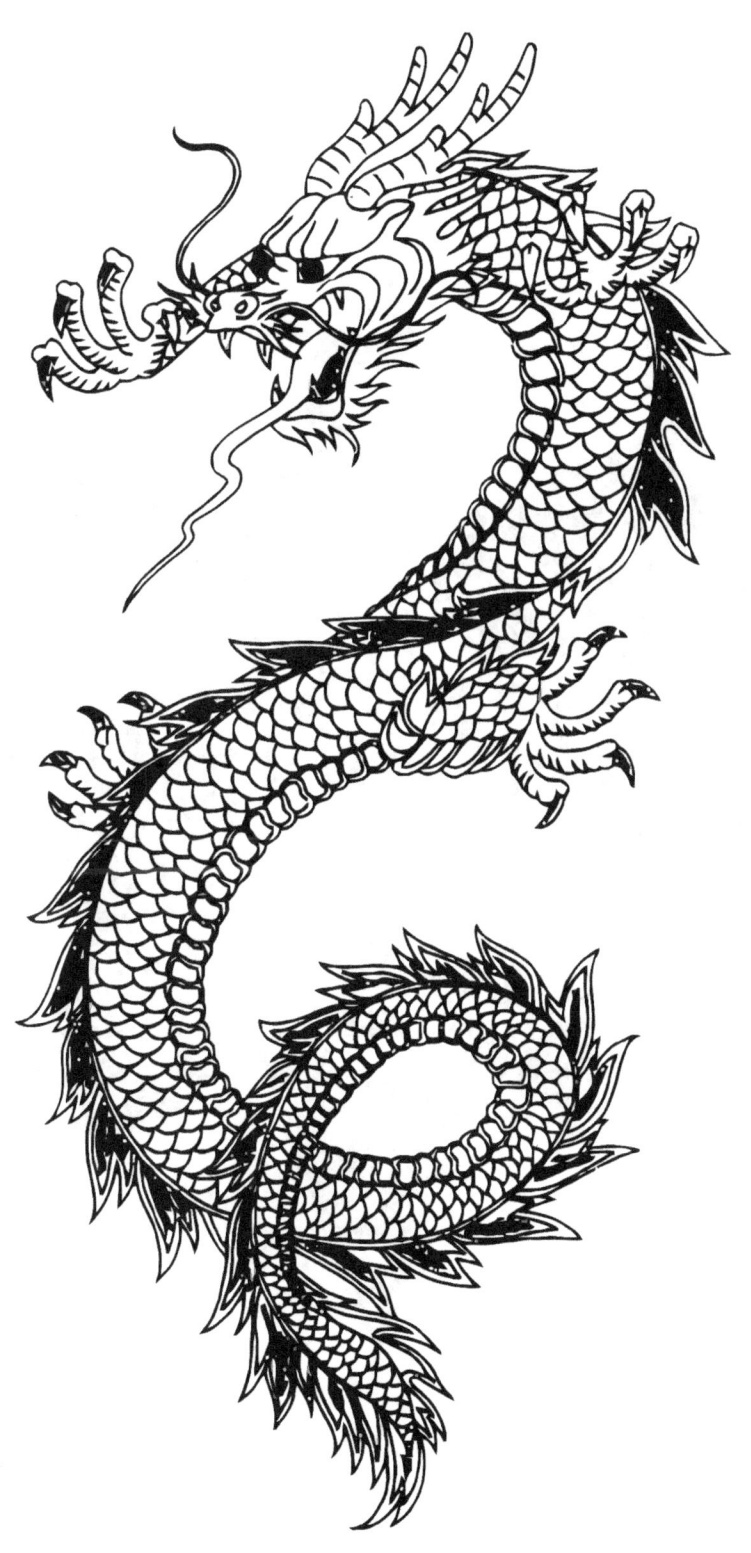

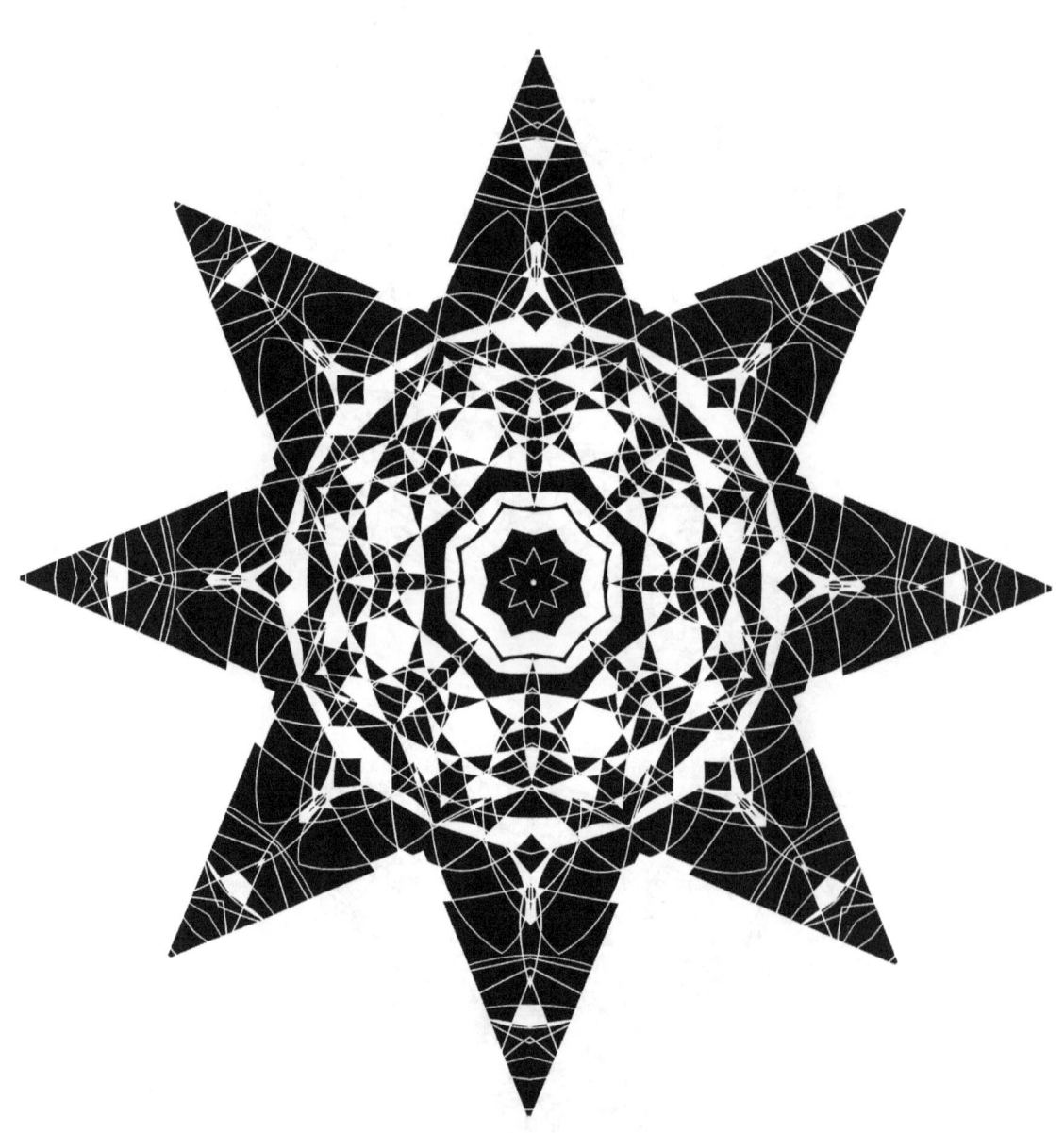

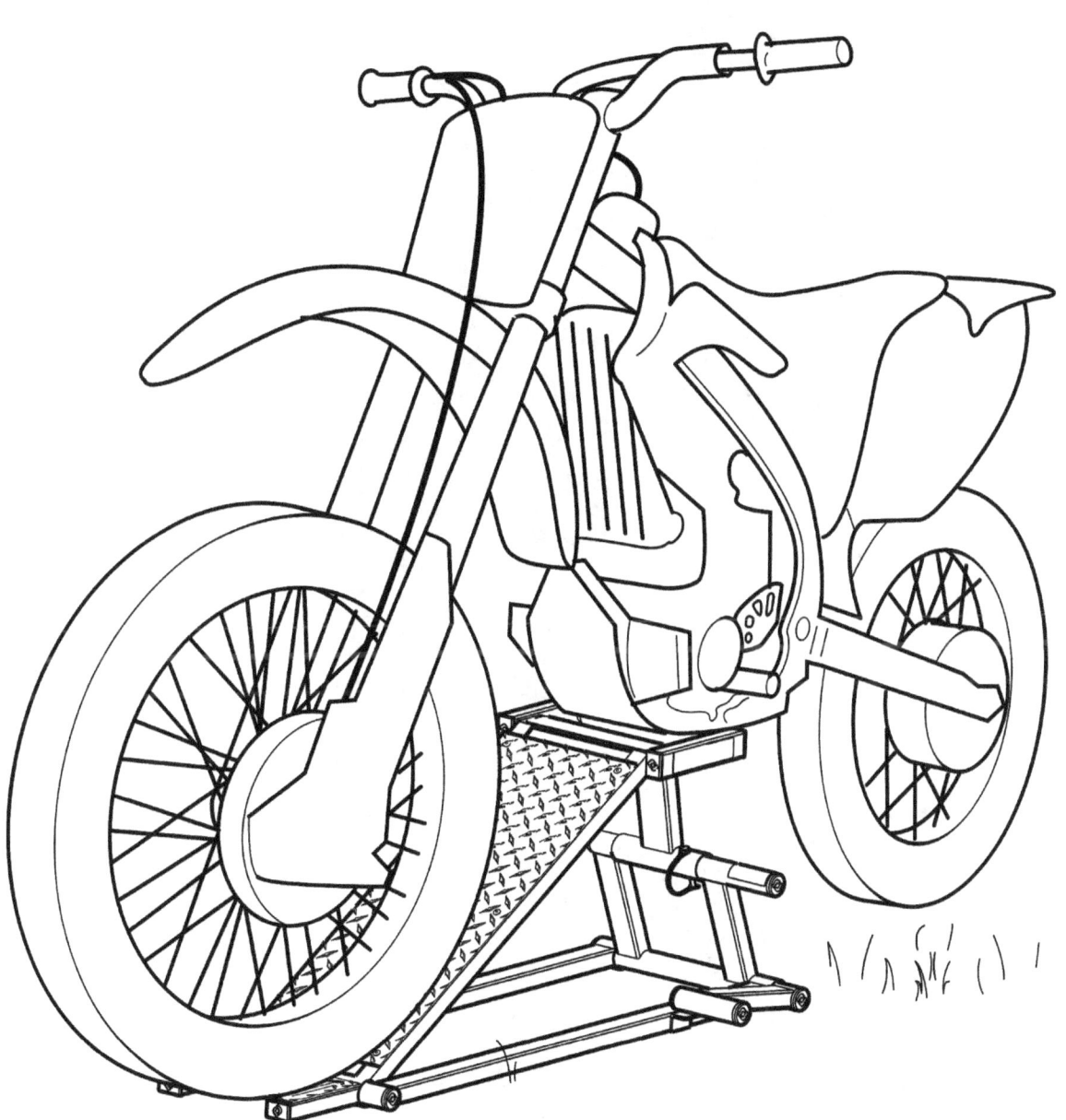

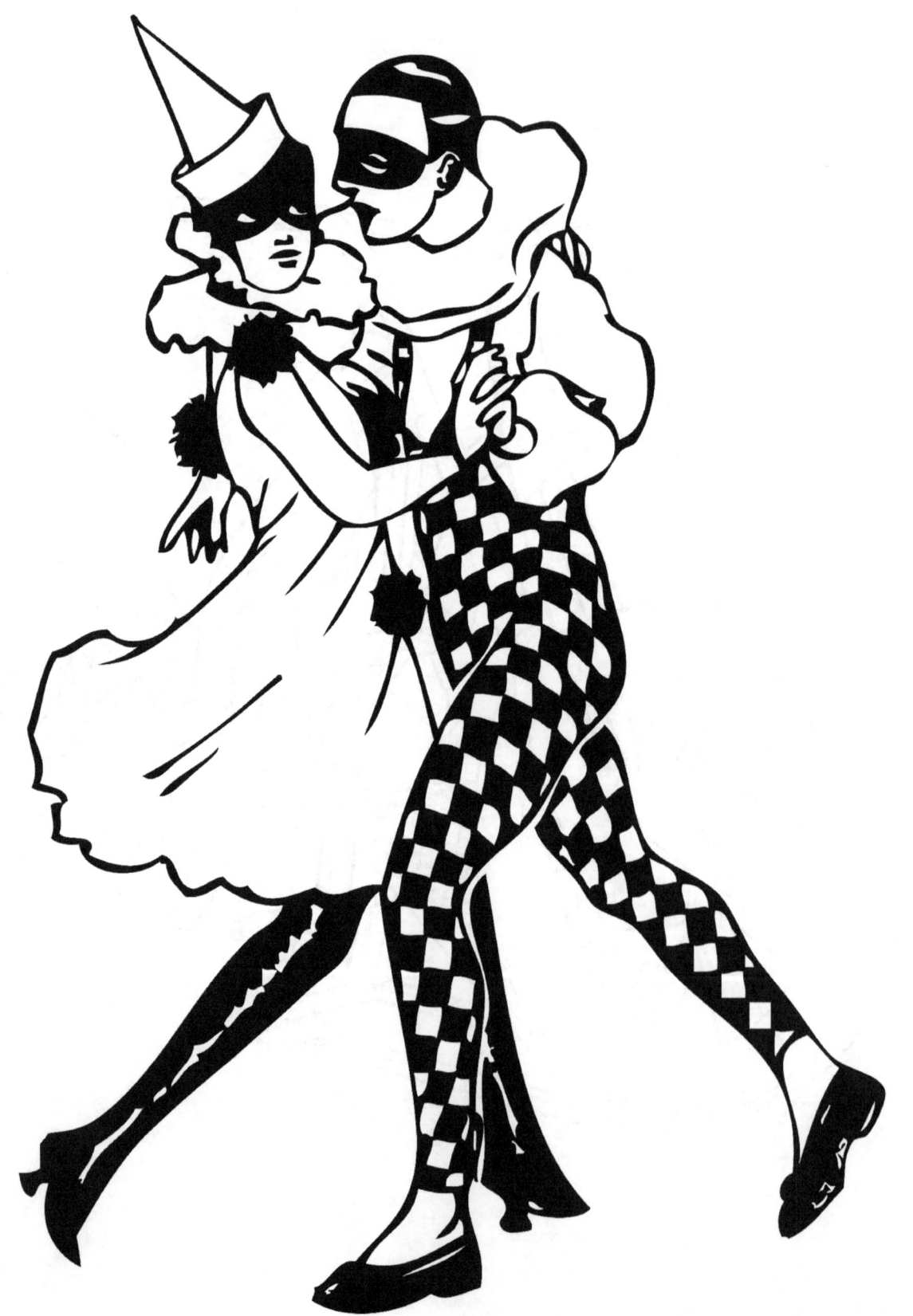

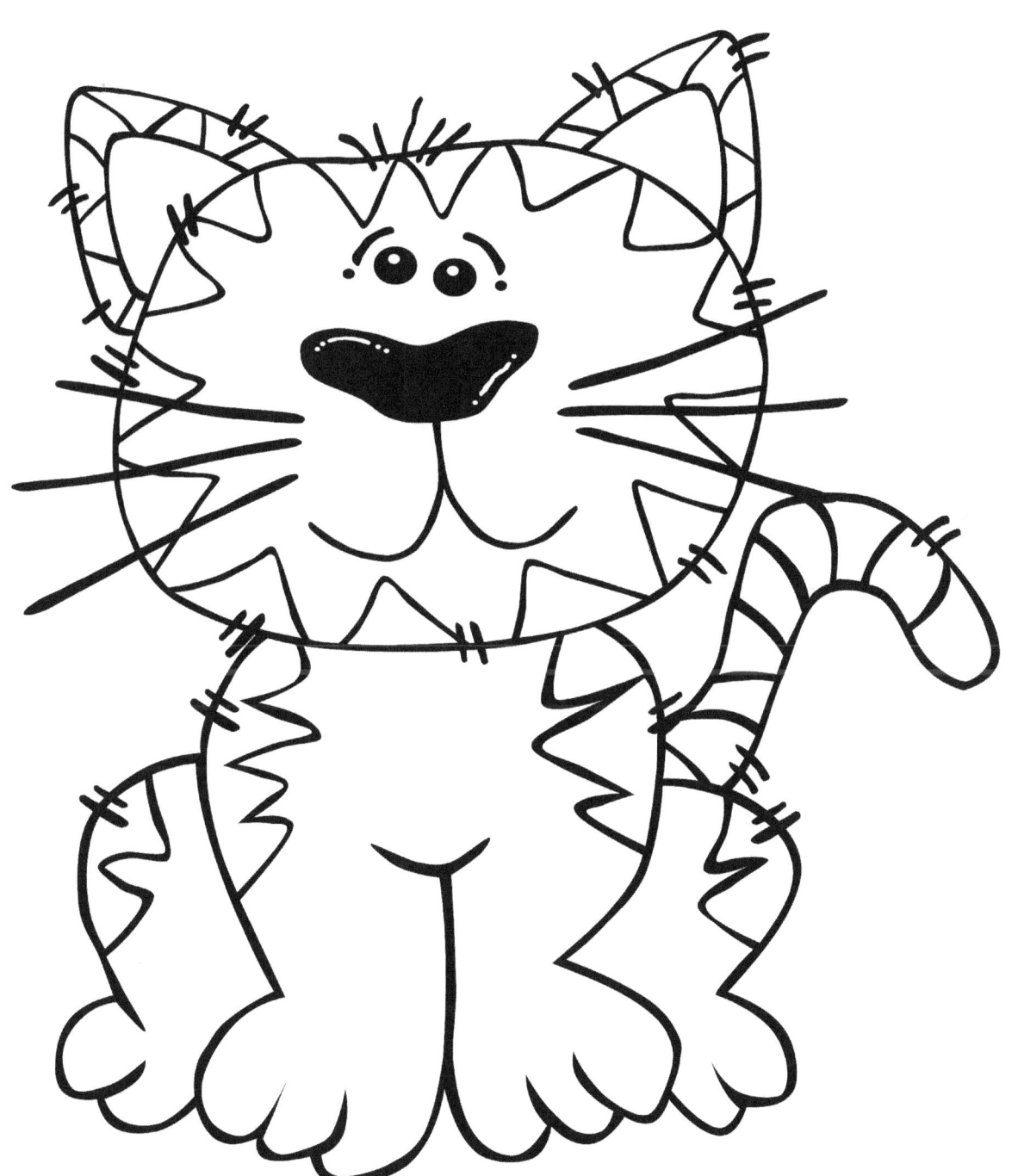

www.ingramcontent.com/pod-product-compliance
Lightning Source LLC
Chambersburg PA
CBHW080644190526
45169CB00009B/3502